MOMMA LOVES YOU

Written and Illustrated by

Katie Hook

NEW YORK

MOMMA LOVES YOU

© 2016 Katie Hook

Published in New York, New York, by Morgan James Publishing. Morgan James and The Entrepreneurial Publisher are trademarks of Morgan James, LLC. www.MorganJamesPublishing.com

The Morgan James Speakers Group can bring authors to your live event. For more information or to book an event visit The Morgan James Speakers Group at www.TheMorganJamesSpeakersGroup.com.

A **free** eBook edition is available with the purchase of this print book.

CLEARLY PRINT YOUR NAME ABOVE IN UPPER CASE
Instructions to claim your free eBook edition:
1. Download the BitLit app for Android or iOS
2. Write your name in **UPPER CASE** on the line
3. Use the BitLit app to submit a photo
4. Download your eBook to any device

ISBN   9781630474959   paperback
ISBN   9781630474966   eBook
Library of Congress Control Number:
2014920246

Cover Design by:
Chris Treccani
www.3dogdesign.net

Interior Design by:
Chris Treccani
www.3dogdesign.net

In an effort to support local communities, raise awareness and funds, Morgan James Publishing donates a percentage of all book sales for the life of each book to Habitat for Humanity Peninsula and Greater Williamsburg.

Get involved today, visit
www.MorganJamesBuilds.com

Habitat for Humanity®
Peninsula and
Greater Williamsburg
Building Partner

Dedication

For my family; you are a constant reminder of God's goodness.

The night sky lit up with bright stars. Momma rocked baby David in her favorite rocking chair. After he yawned and said, *"Night, night,"* he laid his head on Momma's shoulder and fell fast asleep. She snuggled him close and sang a song.

"Momma loves you, but not more than Jesus.
Momma loves you, but not more than Him.
For He is Creator and Maker of you.
Make Him the LORD of your life.
He loves you.
We love you, too!"

David grew big and strong. Momma and Daddy loved David and helped him learn about Jesus. Daddy taught him how to throw a ball and fill his toy truck up with dirt. Momma showed him how to eat with a spoon and write his name.

One day, Momma said to David, *"We are going to have a new baby soon."* David was excited. He wanted a baby brother, but Momma said, *"You are going to have a baby sister."* David was sad for a moment, but the first time he held his newborn baby sister, he loved her dearly.

Momma tucked baby Elizabeth in a warm blanket and sat down in her favorite rocking chair. As she rocked her, Momma sang and prayed over her little girl. Daddy and David watched and prayed from the open door.

"Momma loves you, but not more than Jesus.
Momma loves you, but not more than Him.
For He is Creator and Maker of you.
Make Him the LORD of your life.
He loves you.
We love you, too!"

One night, David was sitting alone on the couch. He knew he had done some things wrong and sinned against God. He prayed and asked Jesus to forgive him. Then he asked Jesus to be his LORD.

David told Momma and Daddy about praying to Jesus. They were very happy for him. The truth in the song Momma had sung many times to him had happened. Jesus was David's LORD.

Momma was so happy to see David read his Bible. He learned from God's Word that there were many people who didn't know Jesus. He prayed for them.

Four years later, Momma had a surprise for David and Elizabeth. *"You are going to have a baby sister."* Elizabeth was thrilled to have a sister, but David was sad. He wanted a baby brother, but the first time he saw his newborn sister, he loved her dearly.

Momma sang to baby Caroline.

"Momma loves you, but not more than Jesus.
Momma loves you, but not more than Him.
For He is Creator and Maker of you.
Make Him the LORD of your life.
He loves you.
We love you, too!"

Elizabeth loved her big brother. It was always exciting to set up a tent in the living room and have a *"camp-in"*. Elizabeth did lots of things that David enjoyed doing just to be near him. She even learned to fish.

As Elizabeth grew, Momma and Daddy kept teaching her about Jesus. Her favorite hobby was cooking with Momma in the kitchen. Elizabeth felt happy when Momma nicknamed her, *"my little chef!"*

One night, David told Elizabeth about Jesus and how much He loved her. Elizabeth asked Jesus to be her LORD. She realized she had done some things wrong and had sinned against God. She asked Jesus to forgive her. David prayed with her. Momma and Daddy were so happy. Momma, Daddy, David, and Elizabeth knew they would see Jesus one day in heaven. They were all happy.

Elizabeth and David told baby Caroline about Jesus. They pray that Caroline would one day make Jesus the LORD of her life. Momma sings to her every night.

"Momma loves you, but not more than Jesus.
Momma loves you, but not more than Him.
For He is Creator and Maker of you.
Make Him the LORD of your life.
He loves you.
We love you, too!"

Momma Loves You

By: Katie Hook

Printed in the USA
CPSIA information can be obtained
at www.ICGtesting.com
JSHW072020140824
68134JS00041B/3724